Holidays

A WORLD OF HOLIDAYS

THANKSGIVING

A WORLD OF HOLIDAYS

THANKSGIVING

Marilyn Miller

RSVP

**RAINTREE
STECK-VAUGHN**

PUBLISHERS

The Steck-Vaughn Company

Austin, Texas

Published by Raintree Steck-Vaughn Publishers, an imprint of Steck-Vaughn Company

Library of Congress Cataloging-in-Publication Data

Miller, Marilyn F.
    Thanksgiving / Marilyn Miller.
        p.   cm. — (A world of holidays)
    Includes bibliographical references and index.
    Summary: Examines the traditions and celebrations associated with the holiday of Thanksgiving.
    ISBN 0-8172-4612-6
    1. Thanksgiving day—Juvenile literature.
[1. Thanksgiving Day.   2. Holidays.]   I. Title.
II. Series.
GT4975.M57   1998
394.2649—dc21   97-27926
                                           CIP
                                            AC

Printed in Spain
Bound in United States
1 2 3 4 5 6 7 8 9 0 01 00 99 98 97

Note to reader: Plymouth Colony is the current spelling for the place that the Pilgrims in Massachusetts first settled. The old spelling "Plimoth" is used today for the name of the museum and the re-created village at Plimoth Plantation.

ACKNOWLEDGMENTS

Editors: Su Swallow, Pam Wells
Design: Raynor Design
Production: Jenny Mulvanny

The author and Publishers would like to thank the following for permission to reproduce photographs:

Cover © Gary Chowanetz/StockMarket
Title page Pamela Hamilton/Image Bank

page 6 (top) Simon Harris/Robert Harding Picture Library (bottom) Zefa Pictures   **page 7** Robert Harding Picture Library   **page 8** (top right) Getty Images (bottom left) Trip/Viesti   **page 9** Private Collection/Bridgeman Art Library   **page 10** Historical Society of Pennsylvania, USA/Bridgeman Art Library   **page 11** (top right) National Portrait Gallery, Smithsonian Institute/Bridgeman Art Library (bottom left) Trip/Peter Bennett, Viesti   **page 12** (top left) Trip/ Viesti (bottom left) Hulton Getty Images

page 13 Trip/Viesti   **page 14** (top left) Trip/Ginny Ganong Nichols, Viesti (main image) Private Collection/Bridgeman Art Library   **page 15** (top) R Bamber (bottom left) Tony Stone (bottom right) Tony Stone   **page 16** (left) Kenneth Redding/Image Bank (right) Zefa Pictures   **page 17** (top) Luis Castaneda/Image Bank (bottom) Rob Van Petten/Image Bank   **page 18** (left) Trip/Viesti (right) Trip/Viesti   **page 19** (top) Pamela Hamilton/Image Bank (bottom) Trip/Viesti   **page 20** (top) Craig Aurness/Robert Harding Picture Library (bottom) Ron Watts/Robert Harding Picture Library   **page 21** (top) Robert Estall Photo Library (bottom) Alain Evrard/Robert Harding Picture Library   **page 22** (top) Trip/Viesti (bottom) Trip/Viesti   **page 23** Trip/Viesti   **page 24** (left) Panos Pictures (right) Jon Spaull/Panos Pictures   **page 25** Christine Osborne Pictures   **page 26/27** Trip/H Rogers **page 28 and 29** Anthony King/Medimage

Contents

The Meaning of Thanksgiving

Late autumn! The air turns crisp, and it grows dark earlier. In the United States and Canada, one source of light in the time before Christmas is Thanksgiving.

As the leaves on the trees in Vermont change color, thoughts turn to Thanksgiving.

EARLY HARVEST FESTIVALS

The first Thanksgivings that were celebrated in the United States were harvest festivals. All over the world, such festivals or holidays have been held from the earliest times. On these days people gathered to give thanks that they had enough food for the coming year. Thanksgiving Day in the United States probably grew out of harvest festivals that English colonists had seen before coming to the United States. In both Canada and the U.S., Thanksgiving still takes place in the late autumn, after the crops have been harvested. On this day, which is now an official holiday, people give thanks for the blessings of the past year.

The flavors of the very first Thanksgiving feasts can be tasted today in Massachusetts.

6

FAMILIES GATHER TOGETHER

Thanksgiving is traditionally a family day, celebrated with special turkey dinners and happy reunions. Children especially love this holiday filled with delicious food. In the days before Thanksgiving, airports and roads are jammed as family members travel to be together. Friends are often invited to share the holiday dinner. Although this joyful holiday reminds many of the good smells of cooking and baking, it has a serious side. This national holiday is also a day for church services and prayer.

Turkey is in the center of most Thanksgiving tables!

The First Thanksgiving in America

The very first Thanksgiving was celebrated by 39 English settlers after they arrived at Berkeley Plantation on the James River in Virginia, in 1619.

At the first Thanksgiving, the English settlers offered prayers of thanks for their safe arrival in America.

A replica of the *Mayflower*, which sailed from Plymouth, in England, to America in 1620.

THE PILGRIMS CELEBRATE IN NEW ENGLAND

On this first Thanksgiving, the settlers prayed but did not feast. But a bigger celebration that is often believed to be the first Thanksgiving took place in New England.

In 1620, 102 English settlers on the sailing ship *Mayflower* landed at what is now Plymouth, Massachusetts, in New England. The place where they settled was named Plymouth Plantation. A harsh winter, hunger,

An artist painted this picture of the first Thanksgiving feast nearly 300 years after the event.

and sickness killed about half of the settlers during that first year. By the summer of 1621, the Pilgrims' lives were better. Governor William Bradford expected a plentiful corn harvest. He arranged a harvest festival for the Pilgrims to rejoice together.

The Pilgrims celebrated for three days. The men shot turkeys, geese, ducks, and deer. The women cooked and prepared the food. Other foods were smoked eel, clams, herbs, and rye bread. About 90 Massachuset Indians were invited to share the feast. They brought five deer to add to the meal. There were games of skill and chance, and target-shooting with guns and bows and arrows. The Indians performed some of their dances, and Captain Miles Standish inspected his troops. It was a day to be remembered for everyone!

A Public Holiday

The other American colonies liked the Pilgrim custom of celebrating a day of thanksgiving for good harvests. So they began celebrating this day, too.

TWO SEPARATE THANKSGIVINGS

The Americans had other reasons to be happy. During the Revolutionary War (1775–1783), they set aside eight days in thanks for their military victories against the British. After the war, General George Washington became the first President. In 1789, he named November 26 as a day of national thanksgiving. But during the same year, church leaders set aside the first Thursday in November as a day to give thanks. So Americans had at least two separate Thanksgiving Days!

At the Battle of Princeton, General Washington led his troops to victory against the British in 1777.

A PRESIDENT DECIDES THE DATE

Different states also celebrated Thanksgiving on different days. The editor of a popular women's magazine, Sarah Josepha Hale, decided to do something about the confusion. For more than 30 years, she asked American Presidents to make Thanksgiving Day a national holiday. Finally, in 1863, President Abraham Lincoln ordered that the last Thursday in November should be observed as a special day of national thanksgiving.

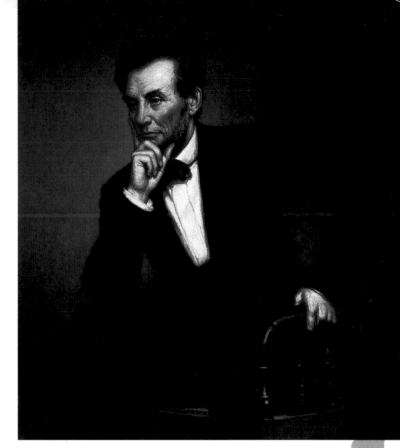

It was Abraham Lincoln who finally set the date for Thanksgiving.

ONE THANKSGIVING FOR EVERYONE

In 1939, President Franklin Roosevelt set the date for Thanksgiving one week earlier. He wanted to add another shopping week before Christmas. But some states kept the old date for Thanksgiving. So two years later, Congress changed Thanksgiving back to the fourth Thursday of November and made it a national holiday.

Canadians celebrate Thanksgiving, too. Their Thanksgiving Day falls on the second Monday in October.

Americans celebrate two important holidays at the end of the year.

11

Bring on the Parade!

Parades have long been a part of the Thanksgiving celebrations. The biggest Thanksgiving spectacle of all is in New York City. Millions of people watch a fantastic parade on television. It is organized by Macy's, the world's largest department store.

DRESSING UP!

Macy's Thanksgiving Day Parade started in the 1920s. Many of Macy's workers were new immigrants from countries in Europe. These workers had happy memories of holiday festivals in Europe. So they decided to hold a public celebration on Thanksgiving Day. What better way to share in the holiday spirit than a lively, colorful parade? Marchers dressed as cowboys and cowgirls, knights in armor, giants, and clowns. There were floats, bands, and 25

animals borrowed from the zoo. The first parade was a great success.

GIANT BALLOONS

The wild animals in the parade frightened some of the children watching. So animal balloons were put in their place. The giant balloons are inflated with an air-and-helium mixture and float high above the crowd. Giant balloons such as Dino the Dinosaur, Dudley the Dragon, Sonic the Hedgehog, and other popular characters mingle with oddities such as a 33-foot (10-m) ice cream cone! Each year the parade ends with Santa Claus' arrival at Macy's on his own float. His arrival marks the start of the Christmas season. Bands from high schools all over the country march in the parade.

Children, wrapped up against the cold, watch the Macy's parade in 1961.

▶ A Bart Simpson balloon towers above the crowd in this Thanksgiving Day Parade.

More Turkey, Please!

In the United States and Canada, Thanksgiving would not be Thanksgiving without turkey. For their Thanksgiving the Pilgrims feasted on wild turkeys cooked over an outdoor fire. They had hunted the turkeys in the surrounding woods.

An American artist's painting of a Thanksgiving turkey shoot.

TURKEYS ON THE FARM

Today the turkeys on most Thanksgiving tables are White Hollands, whose feathers are all white. White Holland turkeys are raised on farms in fenced fields or pens. Farm turkeys have larger heads than wild turkeys. But wild turkeys can do something that farm turkeys cannot do. Wild turkeys can fly!

14

THE TURKEY'S IN THE OVEN

On the holiday morning, kitchens fill with delicious smells of turkey roasting and pies baking in the oven. For many North Americans, Thanksgiving is their favorite "food holiday."

Big birds like turkeys need a lot of time to roast. Even small turkeys take about three hours to cook. The largest turkeys can weigh 24 pounds (11 kg) and need about five hours to be done. If the turkeys are filled with stuffing, they are roasted a little longer. Turkey is traditionally served with mashed potatoes, squash, and, especially, cranberry sauce.

Before everyone eats, someone usually says a prayer at the table. There is no special Thanksgiving prayer, but in their prayers people give thanks for the blessings of the past year.

ALL THE PIES YOU CAN EAT

On Thanksgiving people usually eat until they are so full that they cannot

Thanksgiving turkey would not be the same without the cranberry sauce!

take one more bite! But before that happens, they leave a little space for Thanksgiving pies, made of fruit or mincemeat. But the traditional Thanksgiving pie is pumpkin pie. The Pilgrims learned about pumpkins from the Indians. They filled the pumpkin shell with milk, sugar, and spices. Then they baked it in the fireplace. Today pumpkin pie is made with a pastry crust.

A feast for everyone, from oysters and turkey (left) to pumpkin pie (below).

🦃 Touchdown! 🦃

Since the first Pilgrim Thanksgiving, Americans have loved to fill the day with holiday fun. In some parts of the country, young men used to light bonfires on the tops of hills. In New York City, it was the custom before World War II for people to picnic in parks and then dance until dawn at elegant balls.

Lining up to play. Football (left) and marching bands (below) are a traditional part of the Thanksgiving celebrations.

FOOTBALL IN NEW YORK CITY

Thanksgiving and football seem to "go" together. By the early 1890s, New York City was the site for the annual Thanksgiving Championship game between the two best college teams. As many as 40,000 people watched the game. Unlike today, people really dressed up for this game. Boxes on the sidelines provided the best view of the action.

16

OLD RIVALS

Some college football teams play each other every Thanksgiving. Since 1894, the University of Texas has played Texas A & M every Thanksgiving. The University of Texas has won 66 of these games! Other college teams have played against each other during the holiday since the 1950s. These games used to be on the holiday. But now most of these Thanksgiving college football games are played on the Saturday following Thanksgiving. College players are not the only ones on the football field during the holiday. High school football teams also play against their local rivals

Every team looks to its cheerleaders — and its mascot — to help them win, especially at Thanksgiving.

during the holiday. At the end of each of these games, the winning team often gets an award.

The winning team will enjoy this Thanksgiving even more!

17

🦃 A Special Thanksgiving 🦃

Thanksgiving in Plymouth, Massachusetts, where the first English Pilgrims landed, is very special. Every year thousands of visitors come to share in the holiday events.

FIFTY-ONE PILGRIMS

On Thanksgiving morning, excited crowds line the street to watch the march from Plymouth Rock to church. Each of the 51 marchers wears a costume. They stand for the men, women, and children who survived the first winter in the Plymouth Plantation colony. (See page 8.) Inside the church, worshipers sing psalms from the Book of Psalms in the Bible. The psalms praise God and thank him for his goodness. They are the same psalms that the Pilgrims sang.

1990s "Pilgrims" in Plymouth, Massachusetts, relive the Thanksgiving of more than 350 years ago.

A TON OF TURKEY

Afterward, Thanksgiving dinner is served to the public inside Memorial Hall. This dinner is based on the first Pilgrim holiday meal. It is served not once, but four times in a row, so that many people can eat. By the end, they will have eaten about 1,000 pounds (450 kg) of turkey! The dinner ends with Indian pudding, made with cornmeal and sweetened with sugar and molasses.

LIVING HISTORY

Today, Plimoth Plantation is an outdoor museum — open from April to November — which re-creates the life of a Pilgrim village of 1627. Actors in costume perform many of the original Pilgrim activities, such as planting crops.

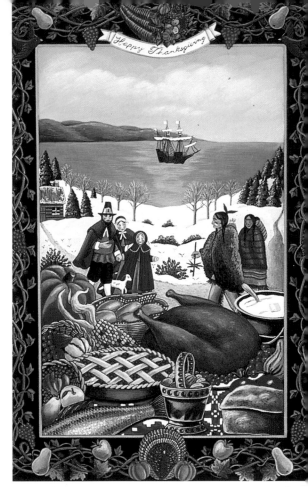

The story of Thanksgiving is told on a greeting card.

The meeting of Pilgrims and Indians is re-enacted at the Plimoth Plantation Museum.

19

Northern Lights

In Canada, Thanksgiving is a family holiday, just as it is in the United States. But this northern neighbor gets more than one month headstart on the festivities. Canadians celebrate their Thanksgiving in October.

THE WAR IS OVER!

In 1763, British colonists in Canada had a lot to cheer about. The French and Indian War between the British and the French, which began in 1755, was over. At the end of the war, France handed Canada over to England. The people of Halifax,

Thanksgiving in Canada is an opportunity to give thanks for the harvest (above). It is also the time to close up the lakeside log cabins for the winter (below).

Nova Scotia, decided to remember this happy event by a day of Thanksgiving. Over the years the custom spread to other parts of Canada. The holiday was not a religious holiday but a national day of giving thanks for the blessings of the past year.

In 1957, Parliament said that people all over Canada should celebrate Thanksgiving on the same day, the second Monday in October. And that is what they have done ever since.

Thanksgiving celebrations in Canada are like those in the United States, but French Canadians may have ham or lamb instead of turkey. In the country you might find *la tourtière*, a pie of many layers filled with potatoes, rabbit or hare, and partridge or pheasant!

A "Mountie" stands guard in front of Canada's Parliament buildings in Ottawa.

A French-style castle-hotel overlooks the city of Quebec, in the part of Canada that is French-speaking.

21

Thanksgiving in Europe

Flowers and ribbons fit for any festival!

Other countries in the world have special days for giving thanks in the autumn. In the Czech Republic, October 28 is a day of thanksgiving. On this day, people go to church to give thanks for the harvest. The next day they dance and feast.

TWO DAYS TO CELEBRATE!
The Czechs have two harvest celebrations. The church part of the holiday is called *Posviceni*. The joyous day of dancing and feasting that follows is called *Obzinky*. After the harvest is completed, farmworkers make wreaths of rye, wildflowers, straw, or sheaves of wheat. These wreaths are placed on the heads of the

Children dance in traditional Czech costume — this time in Texas!

prettiest girls. Next, they all make their way to the owner of the land, to present him with a wreath. Then he invites the farmworkers to dance and feast. And what happens to the wreath? The landowner usually saves it in a place of honor until the next harvest.

A SPECIAL TREAT!

Guests at the feast are usually served roast goose and roast pig. Many people also love to eat *sauerkraut* — a dish of shredded, pickled cabbage. And there is another special treat, pastries called *Kolache*. These are filled with jam, sweetened cottage cheese, or poppy seeds. Delicious!

Making *Kolache* is a serious business — but eating them is great!

🦃 Festivals in Africa 🦃

In Sierra Leone, in Central Africa, Thanksgiving can be celebrated at any time during the year. During this day people of every religion sit down at a feast. They thank the spirits of their dead ancestors for all the good things that have happened.

INVITATION TO THE FEAST

The people of Sierra Leone call their Thanksgiving feast the *Awoojoh*. The day begins with a family visit to the graves of ancestors. There, the family invite the dead to the feast.

Lost in thought. Thanksgiving festivals everywhere are a time to remember the good things that have happened.

Bright cottons are fit for any feast day.

Afterward, the family returns home. Inside they settle any family quarrels. Only then can they sit down at the holiday feast. The main dish is a stew. The eldest person in the family speaks to the spirits of the dead. Some of the stew is kept for the dead relatives. Their serving is thrown to the vultures, which feed off it. The people believe that the vultures are really the souls of their dead relatives come back to Earth.

24

The end of a church service in Freetown, the capital of Sierra Leone. Africans who are Christians give thanks at their own harvest festivals.

FLOWERS AND GREEN PALMS

Thanksgiving is also a holiday in Cameroon, in Africa. But it has a special African flavor all its own.

Christians in Cameroon celebrate Thanksgiving on September 8. Christians are followers of Jesus Christ. On this day they give thanks for having been told the story of Jesus. Who told them the story? They were told by missionaries, people who spread the teachings of their religion to others. The Christians of Cameroon call their Thanksgiving *Evamelunga.* This means "the taking away of the burden of sin." A sin is any act that is felt to be bad, like telling lies or cheating.

On Thanksgiving morning, churches are decorated with flowers and green palms. Families dress in brightly colored clothes. A drum beats out an invitation for everyone to come to the meeting in the church. People enter the church singing. During the meeting, people tell why they are grateful. A young boy is grateful because he is now able to read the Bible. A father is glad because his fear of witchcraft has vanished. They all thank God that they have heard the story of Jesus. After the meeting, there is feasting and singing into the night.

25

Celebrating in School

Thanksgiving is a holiday for the family. In the United States, the main event is the meal, which is shared at home, but many schoolchildren enjoy the fun of the holiday at school, too!

PLAYS AND PARTIES

Putting on a play about Thanksgiving is a good way to learn history and to have some fun! Teachers and children make costumes. For the Pilgrims, there are bonnets for the women, and

Thanksgiving can be an opportunity to celebrate other historical events, such as Independence Day.

Dressed up for the story of the first Thanksgiving.

A church service to celebrate a harvest festival.

hats and shoe buckles for the men. But there is competition to play the part of the American Indians — a favorite role with many in the class.

In some schools, they make a large paper turkey, and each child writes on it to say what they are thankful for. Real turkey may be served for the school lunch, and with it, cranberry relish that the children may have made themselves. It may be sour, or sweetened with orange juice and sugar, or flavored with walnuts. And everyone leaves room for some delicious apple or pumpkin pie!

GIFTS FOR OTHERS

In Great Britain schoolchildren give thanks for the year's harvest at their autumn festival. They may bring gifts of food and flowers that will later be given to people in their community. The same happens in some schools in the United States, where children bring gifts of canned and fresh food to fill baskets for families in need.

Thanksgiving, like many other holidays, is a chance to remember the past and to be thankful for the good things that have happened during the year.

☗ Let's Celebrate! ☗

Join in the Thanksgiving celebrations! Try making a turkey table decoration for any special meal, and some delicious cranberry delight to eat with your turkey.

MAKING A PINECONE TURKEY

2. Color the leaves in bright shades.
3. Cut the leaves out carefully.
4. Set the pinecone on its side. It will be the body of the turkey.
5. Glue the leaves to the bottom of the pinecone to look like feathers. Use the picture below to help you.
6. Glue the walnut to the top of the pinecone to make the turkey's head. You might need to snap off a few scales to make the walnut fit.

Materials:
• a dry pinecone
• one walnut in its shell
• colored cardboard or stiff paper
• crayons or felt-tipped pens
• craft glue
• safe scissors

Directions:
1. Draw six leaf shapes on your paper. You can trace around the edge of a real leaf.

MAKING A CRANBERRY DELIGHT

Ask an Adult to Help You.

Things you will need:

- 1 envelope of unflavored gelatin
- 2 cups of very hot water
- 1⅓ cups (315 g) of whole cranberry sauce, drained
- ½ cup chopped walnuts
- 1 cup low-fat sour cream
- vegetable oil
- 2 large bowls

Directions:
1. **Ask an adult** to help with this. Pour the hot water into the bowl. Dissolve the gelatin in the water. Stir in the cranberry sauce.
2. Chill until the cranberry gelatin has slightly thickened.
3. Stir in the nuts. **Warning!** Some people are allergic to nuts. This recipe can be made without nuts.
4. With a spoon, fold the sour cream into the cranberry gelatin.
5. Wipe the inside of a clean bowl with a little vegetable oil, using a paper towel. Pour the mixture into the bowl and chill until set. Now enjoy eating your cranberry delight!

Glossary

ancestors Relatives that are long dead.

ancient Very old.

celebrate To show that a certain day or event is special.

celebration Way of celebrating a special day.

colonist A person who settles in a different country.

float A vehicle with a platform that carries an exhibit in a parade.

immigrants People who come to live in a country permanently.

Pilgrims English colonists who settled in Plymouth, Massachusetts, in 1620.

soul The human spirit — the part that is left when the body dies.

spirits Beings that you cannot see — something like ghosts.

traditional Customary; an old way of doing something.

Further Reading

Bowen, Gary. *Stranded at Plimoth Plantation 1626.* HarperCollins Children's Books, 1994.

Child, Lydia M. *Over the River and Through the Wood.* HarperCollins Children's Books, 1993.

Feller, Caroline. *Thanksgiving: Stories and Poems.* HarperCollins Children's Books, 1994.

Hayward, Linda. *The First Thanksgiving.* Random House Books for Young Readers, 1992.

Licht, Fred. *Shelter the Pilgrim.* Creative Education, 1990.

San Souci, Robert. *N.C. Wyeth's Pilgrims.* Chronicle Books, 1991.

Index